WALKING TO S~~ANTIAGO~~

Christmas '93

Cal —

Sign-posted
and well-trod, it is the way it holds out
a promise at once so positive and
so paradisal that is the lure of it.'
<u>Contradictions</u>

sent with love,
Gaynor x

NEIL CURRY

Walking
to
Santiago

London
ENITHARMON PRESS
1992

First published in 1992
by the Enitharmon Press
36 St George's Avenue
London N7 0HD

Distributed in the USA
by Dufour Editions Inc.
PO Box 449, Chester Springs
Pennsylvania 19425

ISBN 1 870612 13 2 (paper)
ISBN 1 870612 18 3 (cloth)

The paperback edition is limited to 800 copies
and the cloth edition to 25 signed and numbered copies

Set in 10pt Ehrhardt by Bryan Williamson, Darwen
Printed by Antony Rowe Ltd, Chippenham, Wiltshire

For
Natasha and Victoria

ACKNOWLEDGEMENTS

Some of these poems first appeared in the following publications:
*Ambit, Confraternity of St James Bulletin, The Green Book, Iron,
The New Lake Poets, North, Orbis, Owl, Poetry Durham, Poetry Matters,
Poetry Review, Resurgence.*

'Swallows and Tortoises' first appeared in *The Orange Dove of Fiji:
Poems for the World Wide Fund for Nature.*

'Skulls' appeared in *The Poetry Book Society Anthology 1989-90.*

Contents

New Maps for Old

While once they were allowed
Some flighty bits on the side,

Maps now look to be meaning
At its most monogamous:

No cherubs; no Here Be Dragons;
No galleons tilting in the bay.

Holding an increase in fact
To equal an increase in truth,

They ignore the traveller's need
To tell the lie of the land.

The Excavations at Dry Edge

Their houses had been shaped out of the rock itself
on the north face of the bluffs
and in the deep shade of the overhang,
so that abseiling down from the *mesa*
proved to be as hazardous
as climbing up from the canyon bottom.

But once there,
brushing away the dry centuries of blown sand
was like cleaning a kitchen:
wooden dishes on the tables,
pestles, spoons and storage jars;
and a candlestick carved from a single
stem of juniper, with traces of scented beeswax
still hard-set in the bowl.

Their shallow refuse pits
gave evidence of a balanced diet.
And pollen analysis suggested
some previously unknown varieties
of celery and melon. The corn was mostly
yellow dent, with a little red-ear.

Yet nowhere in the vicinity was there a tilth
fit to scratch, let alone farm,
and none of the wherewithal to trade or barter.
What also went unnoticed at first
was the total lack of weapons, totems and toys.

It was only when Bradshaw,
pressing on into the living space,
found porcelain and bone china there
that they paused awhile in their work.

And then the animal paintings on the wall:
antelope, chamois and caribou;
the attention to detail casting doubt
on any suggestion of sympathetic magic:
those white violets clustered in the foreground,
and the frangipani and hibiscus.

The growing sense of intrusion
both men had remarked upon
was to be explained in the third chamber:
the body of a young woman –
not mummified or embalmed,
but simply dried
owing to the high level of aridity.

Her long hair hung down over a shawl of feathers,
and though her skin had yellowed,
even the eyes were still in place;
'only', as Northrop put it,
'the glint of life missing.'

She had on leather, square-toed sandals
and a loose-fitting garment
woven to a texture
of five hundred threads to the inch.

She was sitting on a stool
with her back against the wall.
She had been opening oysters.
And her left hand clasped that knife
that was to become the symbol
of their Travelling Exhibition:
the owl motif inlaid with silver,
the blade of obsidian.

Knowing Your Place

Not far along the road that crosses
Kirkby Moor, there's a stand of sycamore,
A dozen or so, their tops rounded
And buffed by the wind. Then comes the long slow
Slope of Benson's Hill on up to Horrace.

Away to the left, neglect has bewitched
A hawthorn hedge into a camel-train
Of trees climbing against the sky-line.
Horrace is a child's drawing of a house.
A right turn there takes you down to Lowick.

It's a walk I feel I have perfected.
I know the gate where the piebald ponies
Come dribbling down to have their noses rubbed;
Where brambles, as they die, take on the red
Of Indian leather, and where the Coniston Hills

Begin to unfold. One more right there
Brings you in no time to a tarn: Nut Hollow, or
Knottallow? No one seems sure. But a place
Is its own mind, and to know it truly
Is like knowing a poem: it isn't always

What the words mean that matters, but what is heard
In the silences – in the tension that exists
Between the pulls of memory and feeling.
From now on it is the sound of running water
That will be with me all the way down

To Newbiggin; to a farmhouse sheltered
By a tight fold in the hill, and built
Out of the hill. Making no claims to a view,
It is what is meant by belonging:
A collaboration and an atonement.

By Hubert's Pond

This may be where truth flies:
In the glimpse before recognition;

Before beak touches water;
Before you say, 'No, not a kingfisher,'

And then, as the reed's stave is broken,
'A house martin', – that moment before

The gravitational pull of the word.

A Brief History of Colour

Colour is no more than an optical sensation.
Having no material existence, it is simply
a spectacular event. Viewed from the moon,

without refraction, even the sky is black.
We owe our sunsets here to waterdrops
rinsing the white light of a failing sun

and flushing out those iridescences of lemon
that ripple through darkening skeins of nectarine
towards blood and plumb. Yet none of this

could ever have been captured in natural
umbers with a fistful of charcoal and chalk.
The Roman toga called for Tyrian whelks,

while palettes needed lapis lazuli,
with verdigris of copper and crushed malachite
to give the eye back what the eye can see

when it accepts those stimuli that cause
what we agree to call (say) *green*.
But what of the edges, where the gamut

of visible vibrations fades from view?
What's infra, ultra, may perhaps possess
tinctures comprehended for the question's sake:

the beauty of uncertainties that are absolute.

Swallows and Tortoises

It was the Age of Reason.
And when spring broke in Selborne
And Timothy the tortoise did come forth

And march about, they had a feel
For his pulse, but could not find it;
Bawled at him through a speaking-trumpet
But he appeared not to regard it;

So they dunked him in a tub of water
To see if he could swim, and watched him
Go sinking down to scrabble on the bottom,
quite out of his element, and seemingly

Much dismayed. But what puzzled them most
In Selborne was that Providence
Should squander longevity
On a reptile who relished it so little

As to spend two-thirds of its existence
In a joyless stupor, all but the thread
Of solstitial awareness suspended.

But there are lessons to be learned everywhere,
And as Timothy awoke with the first flight
Of the swallows, might not they too
Have their hybernacula?

And had not Dr Johnson himself seen them
Conglobulate, before throwing themselves
Under water, wherein they would winter
On the bed of the river?

Sometimes Timothy escaped them,
Toddling his carapace out through the wicket:
Pursuits of an amorous kind transporting him
Beyond the bounds of his usual gravity.

A Garland from Persephone

(For Jenny Brown)

'We've been well primrosed,' you said.
And so we had. Hundreds upon hundreds
of them we'd seen. It was that time of year

when the *National Geographic* yellow
of the daffodil gives way to a softer
sulphur. And we're glad of it, knowing

that we will have bowls of buttercup yet
before the blues come: bugle and speedwell
to see us through the great furnace

of the poppy and its sparks of pimpernel;
those reds that tend us into the russet
and final yellows of the fall.

They are a garland drawing us through the days
until our ears strain over the edge
of the year to catch again the trumpet call

of the asphodel, that flower that blows
in the meadows of the underworld; the flower
of Persephone, our Queen of Hell.

Butterflies

Flying worms, Albertus Magnus called them,
    as though unaware that their wings
    were a set of Monet's palettes;
the eyes of the peacock for example:
empurpled browns bleeding into yellow,
       set off by dabs of white
       cleaner than sugar.

And then the rich simplicity of all
    the Blues. Trying to look one up
    in a *Guide* (worse than dictionaries
they are for distractions) you find yourself
entangled in a clap-net of their names:
       April Fritillaries,
       Vernon's Half-mourner.

Adam alone could have dreamt of such things.
    This side Eden, on their bellies
    they crawled, then came that primal soup
and Resurrection's metaphor. Scarce now;
a sometime image for frivolity;
       in closed cabinets, dry
       wings shrivel and fade.

Skulls

(For John Wood)

Down where the swash and backwash of the tide
Had retched up wet entanglements
Of bladder wrack and kelp, the usual
Goitred orange and a single shoe,
We found the dead gannet;

Its intricate, slim wings intact as when
We saw them fold like paper darts
And plunge into the seas round Boreray;
And still with that slight blush of yellow
To the head, like a girl's chin

When you hold a buttercup beneath it.
And I wanted that skull – the great beak
Longer than my longest finger – to put
Beside the hooked and sun-bleached hawk's
On my windowsill.

But lifting it I found the tongue gone
And a thick gruel of maggots
Already on the boil in its gullet.
And I couldn't touch it. We walked off
Talking of flowers instead:

Of the misty and paler-than-harebell blue
Of the sea holly, Crippen's henbane,
And the trumpets of convolvulus
Like the horns of ancient gramophones
Shaped out of porcelain.

But looking back I saw how the wind lifted
One wing and let it flap and fall
Like Ahab's arm when the white whale sounded,
Breached and rolled. And I thought of others
That I had missed out on:

Those oiled razorbills at St Bees,
The rat-gnawed heron on the banks
Of the Nene, and I knew that the only way
To win skulls such as those would have been
To take a knife to them,

Slicing into feather and skin, probing
For the vertebrae, to sever
Cartilage and ligament and cut through
To the bone. It's either that or waiting
For the sea's gift, or the sun's.

Give Us This Day

Standing at his study window,
hearing the nuthatch tap in the acacia,
Francis Kilvert knew
that today was the day
when the people of Langley Burrell would sing
to the sound of their new harmonium.

White, in his Selborne Calendar,
a hundred years before, wrote only, 'Bucks grunt,'
while sometime between,
Dorothy Wordsworth wrote
to Miss Lamb: their tenth cart of coals had arrived;
she and William walked to Butterlip How.

It is, as it was, the Feast Day
of All Saints, part of time's usual *va-et-vient*.
What else have we here?
L.S. Lowry was born,
and the first W.H. Smith bookstall
was opened at London's Euston Station.

The first premium bonds were sold,
and the first hydrogen bomb was exploded.
Orson Welles' Martians
landed in New Jersey,
and in Venice in 1972
Ezra Pound died after a long silence.

As a child I had a Magic
Writing Board with a thin sheet of cellophane
I could doodle on,
and when I felt like it
I'd only to slide the strip of metal down,
and everything I'd scribbled disappeared.

A Last Psalm to David

That time you sang of green pastures
        and still waters,
what a daydream it must all have seemed
    to your ragtail desert rats
    holed-up by Philistines
in the tawny hotlands of Judah.

But now, sir, that you have brought us
        to the sanctum
of Jerusalem, why lie alone
    waiting for death? And why these
    cold shudderings of grief?
If you'd only let them, men would come

dancing to your glory, stamping
        to the sound of
tabrets and the high-sounding cymbals;
    or singing seek to reach out
    and share in your sorrow,
for we too have known our hopes fail

and all our longing in ruins.
        You felt your whole
world had fallen when Yahweh frowned
    on your plans to build a temple,
    forgetting His promise
that your house was to outlast lifetimes.

Lines weak as ours could not bear the
        strain of your sins:
how you murdered that messenger,
    and sent Bathsheba's husband
    to his death so that you
could have her in your bed. Dissidents

you quashed. (O, Absalom, my son.)
    But what endured
was the fable and not the story:
    that while Goliath's spear
    looked like a weaver's beam,
one small boy, with only one small stone

picked from the brook, put down the beast.
    Tell us again
how your harp's song soothed Saul's worst rages.
    Restore in us that fixed heart
    we'll need when we look down
into your long valley of shadows.

For I Will Consider My Dog Toby

Yes, we were sold a pup in Peterborough
and we called you Toby.

You came in a box: a real old
orange box with a lid on,
and little fluffy tufts of hair
sticking out through the slats in the side.
By rights you should have been adorable –
all puppies are. But no, not you.
You hadn't, as the man put it,
when he looked inside,
'travelled very well'. In fact,
you'd puked your price down
by almost half. I suppose we should
have been grateful.

Chewer of chairs, and puddler of carpets,
if your puppihood was predictable,
your teens were traumatic.
Well for me they were at least.
That day I saw you come trotting up the path
with a whole fresh doughnut in your teeth,
I knew then that we were in for trouble.
But couldn't you have just stayed a thief?
Specialised even in it a bit? Did you
have to try to kill van Ashfelt's chickens,
and chase his cows around the field
until you'd damn near buttered all their milk?
And sex. Now I grant you, Toby, that's not
an unreasonable need, but did you
have to keep on raping little Pooch?
I can't tell what you saw in her,
but this I do know – Mrs Vieth herself
is not a pretty lady, and her purple
apoplexy was something I found hard to take.
And what about pinning the postman to the hedge?
And the man who came to read the meter,

just how long had you held him prisoner
in the shed?

You had your good days too of course –
like when we threw a stick into the river
and you ignored it, and came back
with a water-lily in your mouth
and dropped it at your mistress' feet.
There never was such canine gallantry,
and carried off with such panache.
You could do no wrong – not after that.
Compared with you, Sir Walter Raleigh
was a lout. But you were soon back
to your old ways again, and we'd clout you,
and try to shut you in the cellar.
One day I rang the dogs' home and booked you in.
I'd had enough.

But we always forgave you.
That hangdog look that you perfected,
and the big brown doleful eyes. No one could resist.
Yes, beast, I could and would forgive you anything,
except, that is, getting so sick; so sick
that yesterday I had to take you to the vet
and come home again with a full heart
and such an empty lead.

The Days of Creation

'What sceal ic singan?'
'Cwaeþ he: 'Sing me frumsceaft.'

I

In the beginning:

Hearth and sweat
The new art had as
Hearts and wheat.

A new start he had,
Star had new heat.

Then Hades at war,
He at dawn's heart
Was at hand there

And saw that here
Death has a new art;

And what tears he
Shed: a heart-want.

And the water has...

And the heart was...

And the earth was
Without form and void
And the darkness was

And he cwaeþ

Let there be light.

II

And then the waters spoke

No, I'm not at all sure about yesterday.
Today's alright. I mean,
I know where I am today.
I could tell when it began for one thing.
But I'm not sure whether yesterday
ever did begin, or whether I began;
or whether I've always been around;
or what always means for that matter,
or matter...

I could tell when yesterday ended.
That was night.
I'm not sure I liked the night.
It was so dark – not at all
like before there wasn't any light.
But that's one of those things I'm already
Finding it difficult to remember.

Something moved upon my face.
And then there was light. I liked the light.
And I was really happy when it came back again.
That was when today began.
But even today hasn't been altogether good.
I've felt – how can I put it? – *divided*.

It looks as though there's another night coming.

Sometimes I think I know
how the hermit crab is going to feel.

III

Viriditas

And God said:

let there be a process
to be known as photosynthesis,
whereby the pigment chlorophyll,
by means of the radiant energy of the sun
will combine water and carbon dioxide
to produce sugar in the form of glucose,
at the same time giving off oxygen

and the Green Man said:

when I open
my mouth
I utter leaves

IV

For Signs & Seasons

It was Thursday morning already,
and so much still to be done, but
with muesli, toast and tea for breakfast now
He sat awhile and dreamed: of two small boys

playing in a rock pool, teasing the shrimps
and little scuttling things so contentedly
that until they heard it roar they never guessed
a lion, led by a lady all in white

was walking towards them over the hill.
'Let me weigh both your laughters,' she said,
'to tell which is the happier.'
But the scales twisted from her hands

into a scorpion, that bent its tail
as an archer would his bow. Sensing
a tragedy, He shifted in his sleep,
and dreamt up a goat with hoofs like hammers

to stamp on that scorpion; and then of himself,
as the children's father, coming from the house
with a bucket full of water to sluice
the mess away. The water went trickling

over the cobbles and down into the stream,
touching the tail of a trout that jumped,
and startled a ram into leaving its flock,
which caused a bull to abandon its herd

grazing on a cliff overlooking a beach
where two small boys...Enough! It's time for work.
But God, not wanting to forget his dream,
scribbled it across the sky in stars.

V

A Benedicite

'Through the mechanistic operation
of inanimate forces and by the power
of natural selection'
we have:

the cuttlefish, which expands
and contracts bags of yellow, brown,
orange and red pigments embedded in its skin
so as to change colour and blend
in with its background;

and the eye of the common newt,
whose lens, when removed surgically,
will grow again
from the edge of the iris;

and the bombardier beetle,
which defends itself
by squirting out a jet
of noxious benzoquinones
at a temperature of
100 degrees centigrade;

and the male emperor moth
which can detect a female
emperor moth by her smell
at a distance of
eleven kilometres, up wind;

and that series of small peristaltic pumps
arranged along the oesophagus of the giraffe
which enable it to lift water
up to the required height of three metres
when it is standing, head-down
and legs-straddled, drinking;

and the in-built thermometer
of the Snowy Tree Cricket:
add 40 to the number of chirps
it emits in any period of 15 seconds
and you have the exact air temperature
in degrees Fahrenheit.

For these, and so much more,
O, 'Mechanistic Operation',
we give thee thanks.

VI

The Last Pat from the Potter

'I have said enough,' said God.

'I want there to be other tongues
to tell me about the taste
of the honey and the salt;

about the feel of linen to their fingerpads;

about the forest's variations
on my theme of green;

and about onions and soot.

I want to know what someone thinks
about the way the thunder sounds,
the way the waves speak.'

It was the last pat from the potter.

'I have left a little
of myself in this,' said God.
'When it comes to its senses,
I want to hear from it.'

Six Birds

1

A kestrel
lowers itself
down the sky,
like a spider
on a thread.

2

The magpie
lands
with two quick bounces
and a hop,
as though it had meant to.

3

Owl
wears his head in a box
and has to turn the whole thing round,
naturally,
to look out.

4

Peregrine
sits biting its nails,
before biting off
somebody's head.

5

Apprentice sky-writers:
a skein of geese
goes w-wobbling by.

6

Dunlin
run along
stitching the frayed edge of the tide
back to the sand.

Lament for the Last Great Auks

They'd come toddling ashore as usual one year
To nest, in their thousands, on Gerfuglslaga,
Flightless, yet fearless,
And were huddled together
As close as goose pimples, when the whole
Island erupted and exploded; blown
Into a maelstrom of lava, steam and feather
By a volcano that sank it
Hissing beak and rock
Under the cold North Atlantic.

Stateside, meanwhile, ease of living
Meant feather quilts and pillows;
Sent traders to where the sea
Ran white with guano, and the winds
Rank of it a mile out.
That was Funk Island.
And it was a simple business:
Unruffled, the birds
Herded themselves together,
To be lobbed, one by one,
Alive into boiling water.
Even the fires were fuelled with auk fat.

After that they grew so rare
The men of St Kilda
Once held one prisoner for three days
Before bludgeoning it to death,
Convinced it was a witch.

Learning of the very last pair,
Cooler heads in committee rooms,
Mindful for posterity
Had them strangled and stuffed.

The one egg, a mottled green and black,
Being cracked, was no use
So someone stamped on it, and the yoke
Spurted over his boot.

Fieldfares

(For Marjorie White)

Fieldfares are travellers over the fields,
who will stay with us
as long as there's a lace of frost
edging the wall's shadow,
a fresh crust to the grass,
and ice brittle underfoot
in the flanged ruts around gateways.

Serious, northern birds they are,
and watching them prod
and probe in the cold top pasture,
dowdy in their blue-greys,
their browns, their copes and cowls,
puts me in mind of those dour
northern saints: Aidan, Cuthbert, Bede;

powerful men whose muscular
humility thrived
on adversity: Bede breathing
on the ink as it froze
in his horn; Cuthbert
standing, praying, arm-pit deep
in the grey waves off Coldingham.

But no bane was bitter enough:
more books; move on, more;
three onions will suffice to feed
a saint on Inner Farne.
So too, once these becks thaw
and the aconites unfurl,
it will be farewell the fieldfare.

Peregrine

Slipping from its ledge,
it climbs up on the first thermals of the morning,
drifts out in the direction of the bay,
then turns and stops,
its wings hooded like a cobra
as it crouches on the wind and watches me.

An hour ago
there was a moon up there, its edge roughened past full;
somehow I must have lost it at starfade
as the black felt
was silking to cerulean.
The eyes of this peregrine are two new moons.

I have come here
to watch and guard the nest. I am the protector.
The wings clench, and the body rolls and falls,
then one lithe flick
and it's flung itself out of sight
over the far rim of the quarry. Nearby

a grouse clears its throat.
There is a sudden crackle of jackdaws, and a long
line of gulls comes straggling past
like the walking
wounded from some forgotten war.
What follows is not peace but a dead silence.

Walking to Santiago

Pilgrymes and palmers pligted hem togidere
To seke seynt Iames and seyntes in Rome.
Thei went forth in here wey with many wise tales,
And hadden leue to lye al here lyf after.

Roncevaux/Roncesvalles

(For Chris Pilling)

Tear-stained with rain, these beech trees
give a wistful note to the wind,
like that of a distant horn.

Voyez les ports et les détroits passages

This is the frontier of truth
and myth. And truth will have it Crescent
and Cross were not at question here.

Haut sont les puys et les vaux ténébreux

No bold Crusader, Charlemagne;
he'd gone freebooting for the Saracens,
till double-crossed, and piqued, he turned

En douce France s'en repairera le Roi

and trekked back home again – stopping, just once,
so his moody troops could sack
and ransack Basque Pamplona.

Et Sarrasins qui tant sont assemblés

And that's what did it. They were Basques
waiting on the heights of Roncesvalles
while the oriflamme whirled by;

Quatre cents muls chargés de l'or d'Arabe

Basques who dropped down on the baggage-train,
the ox-carts, pack-mules, carpenters
and cooks, and massacred the lot.

'Dieu!' dit le Roi, 'si peineuse est ma vie!'

Such ignominy the chroniclers pooh-poohed.
Losses were few: Anselm, Count Palatine,
and Roland, Warden of the Breton March.

Ci faut la Geste que Turoldus décline.

Xavier

(For Elizabeth McConnell)

Our guide – a Jesuit – met us
under the portcullis,
shock troops of words
sallying out over the drawbridge
of his tongue and routing us
as utterly as would the Basque
that Francis spoke.

How much has changed since he was here?
Not the toothed sierra,
nor the wide, green
valley of the graceful Aragon.
And in the chill shade of the
gateway, out of the midday heat
we shared, I felt,

the same foreboding and relief
climbing the slope beneath
the arrow-ports,
and the stairway winding in towards
St Michael's Tower: last safe
retreat when they were under siege.
Yet an image

of old war engines (arbalists
coiled taut) came to suggest
another kind
of tension that triggered in the mind
and was harder to release.
But Francis braved it; faced the world,
and fired the bolt

that shot him from his fortress home,
eastwards, through pang and storm;
with the valour
to fail, and to take heart from failure.
India. Ceylon. Japan.
He died challenging the darkness
beyond sunrise.

Pamplona

July was once simply
the feria of San Fermin,
himself martyred on the horns of a bull.
These days it's the bust of Hemingway whose scowl
gores the aficionados at the bull-ring.

And down by the river,
as the sun rises, it kindles
a restless chafing of hooves in the dark
fetor of the corral; then you hear the brisk
sound of oboe and drum as the bands come

threading into the square.
The streets seethe: a jostle of white
scarfed in scarlet. Barriers are in place;
and anticipation pulls on the long gap
like a toothache. At the first stroke of eight

the rocket. And the bulls
are out there already running
up Santo Domingo, then swinging left,
horns down, hooking, bunching into the narrows
of the Estafeta. Ahead of them

the headstrong, the macho
and the maverick, charge hell-bent
for the encierro; where in the blanched
heat of the arena, a matador will
lift his bull through bravura de pechos,

then spin it and turn it
in tightening chicuelinas,
the low, slow sweep of the veronica;
the faena and kill: thick embroideries
of blood trailing behind it in the sand.

*   *   *

While on the other side
of the city a plaque: 'Aquí
cayo herido, San Ignacio
Loyola' marks the spot where he fell, wounded:
soldier then – neither Jesuit nor saint,

but sanctified, it seems,
by a ball that splintered his leg
when the armies of France besieged Navarre.
The leg set by surgeons, broken and re-set,
his mind fought at the barriers of pain,

where, moved by stillness, he heard,
in that immaculate silence,
the rallying call to a new standard.
Ad majorem Dei gloriam, he wrote.
A beggar had his cape; the church his sword.

Puente La Reina

'Y desde aquí todos los caminos
a Santiago se hacen uno.'

And three statues greet the four roads.

First, the pilgrim, on his plinth, barefoot,
though that broad-brimmed hat of his,
the stolid staff and capacious cloak
declare him a man of substance.

St James looks ruffled and windblown;
is dusty, anxious-eyed.

While in La Iglesia del Crucifijo
the body of Christ slumps forward
on a Y-shaped,
arm-breaking cross.

There is still a long way to go.

Three statues and four roads. And six arches
to carry this queen of bridges over the river.

Below, a moorhen slowly
prods its way against the stream.
The water is flood-yellow.

A sudden freshet of rain lifts that
savour of new rope from the cobbles.

Storm-clouds have bruised the hills.

On the parapet someone has left
a rose-hip, two blackberries,
an almond and some purple heads of clover.

Once over the bridge
the road veers sharply to the right,
and I know that from now on
I will be 'stepping westward'.

Contradictions

Careless of contradiction, the Camino
accommodates them both: St James the pilgrim,
with scallop shell and staff, walking the world
like one of us; and that other, rough-riding,
sabre-swinging, warrior Santiago,
around whom the heads of Saracens
are bouncing like cherries off a tree.

And then, often as not, in each town
it passes through, two churches: one silent
and swept bare as a meeting house, where the cold
stone comes close to a desert solitude;
and another whose rococo retablo
cataracts down in a gilt extravaganza
of relics and chipped statuary.

Two routes, you might think, but this road
is part of our past, and a matter
of myth: we would not expect to meet up
with the unexpected here. Sign-posted
and well-trod, it is the way it holds out
a promise at once so positive and
so paradisal that is the lure of it.

At the Tomb of Cesare Borgia, Viana

At noon I shared a wineskin with the labourers
In the vineyard, who roared and embraced me
When I got some near my mouth. But this also
Has been one of the dark places of the earth.

When Cesare Borgia, sleek,
Proud and ambitious, came this way,
His horse's hooves were shod with silver,
And even his commode was gold.

Prototype for *Il Principe*, he commandeered
St Peter's Square as a bull-ring once,
And at a banquet for the Pope, his father,
Hired fifty naked courtesans

To crawl about among the feet of the diners.
Sometime cardinal turned poisoner and strangler,
He knew too how the cause of terror can be served
By an act of the simplest brutality.

But on a campaign here, he wildly outpaced
First his troops and then himself, until,
Trapped where those high-rise flats begin,
He was unhorsed, stripped and killed.

Nothing emblazoned now remains. His tomb
Is a slab near the church door, to be trod on.
And there is still the road. In an hour or so
Navarra gives way to La Rioja.

Easter Sunday at Santo Domingo de la Calzada

No thanks to Saint Dominic of the Causeway.
A hard coming I've had of it, foot-sore, soaked
And exhausted, like hundreds of thousands before me,
But the legendary cockerel cooped up
In the Cathedral crows me its greeting.

The legend goes like this: a young pilgrim
Was hanged for a crime that he didn't commit,
But his parents (the Saints preserve us)
Found he was still alive on the gibbet
And went running to tell the magistrate.

He, deep into his supper, scoffed at them.
'Alive?' he said. 'Alive as this roast chicken!'
And the bird, as was only to be expected,
Got up on its toes and promptly crowed.
Rooster and saint are since inseparable.

A lady tells me that this one crowed
Fourteen times during last week's sermon.
Thrice was enough on another occasion.
I'll take the fish tonight. Someone put to death
Last Friday is, I believe, alive again.

Burgos: El Cid

Truth being that which is taken to be true,
I can hardly accept this bronze illusion
of El Mio Cid, El Campeador,
that threatens to gallop over San Pablo Bridge
and away out of Burgos.

A pair of fluted bat-wings round the neck
of the Australian frilled lizard may be proof
of Creation's sense of fun, but as a battle
cloak for our hero seems barely adequate,
even allowing for a sword

that could double as the jib of a dockside crane,
and a beard that niagaras into his saddle-cloth.
I might of course hold a different view
if I'd fought on the shore at Valencia, and heard
his war cry:

En el nombre del Criador e d'apostel santi Yague!
had seen the bloodied, riderless chargers,
the mailed arms hacked off,
and heads in their helmets fall to the ground,
as El Cid de Vivar

slammed Bucar's army back into the waves.
Even when he was dead, they mounted his body
upright on his horse, and the end was the same.
His enemies, believing what they took to be true,
never stood a chance.

At a Station of the Cross

A moment's halt on the line between Burgos
And Palencia. A man crosses the track
With a rose in his mouth. The platform
Is a blaze of marigold and geranium.

We watch a swallow flicker from its nest
Under the eaves and then come swooping down
Past a name that dims the day as it once
Clouded a whole century: *Torquemada*.

My god, the man was born in this place.
The Grand Inquisitor of Spain himself,
Tomas de Torquemada, Prior of the Holy Cross,
Past master of the hoist and rack,

And of the water torture too: pegs of wood
Rammed up the nostrils, the jaws clamped open
And a length of cloth laid over the mouth
So as pint after pint of water

Is poured in, it gags down your throat
And you choke and drown. But never quite, of course:
Dominicans are the most patient of men
And they had a mission to perform. With bells

And incense, and a green cross draped in black,
Their victim, in his yellow sackcloth smock
Embroidered with demons and the flames of hell
Must assist in the last great work of faith,

Watched from under canopies of scarlet and gold
By priests who, serene in their virtue, are shocked
To see so much wickedness in the world.
But we know the world. What shocks me now

Is that he of all men should have been named
After a burned tower – *la tor quemada*. Somewhere
A signal must have changed. Our train shudders,
And we inch off slowly towards Palencia.

Fromista

A dry walk along the side of a slow canal.
Another town. Another plaza mayor.
Another statue. Another saint.

But who's this one who looks to be blessing the world
While riding towards us on a surfboard?
San Telmo, his plinth says. San Telmo?

I've never...No, wait, we've jumbled up the Spanish.
This must be Saint Elmo. He of the fire
That glowed from the harpoons Ahab held.

But what can the patron saint of sailors
Be doing here in the wide wheat-fields of Spain?
My guidebook tells me it's because he was martyred

By having his intestines winched out of him
On a windlass. Dear god, is the imagination
Of man never so fertile as when

We are inflicting pain on one another?

Checks and Balances

What I don't know is why I didn't give up

When the rain fell outside Puente La Reina
And the old road ran into a red quag
Of new roadworks, so that for over a mile
I had to stop every half minute to scrape
Coagulations of sludge from my boots

And when I got lost again and again
Between those yellow crumbling villages
Beyond the Rio Oja, and yet another
Pair of half-starved dogs, lips curled
And snarling, came leaping and gnashing at me

And when my own folly and bravado tempted me
To try and cram two full days' walk into one,
And the last six miles into Burgos
Were a dual carriageway, and the buffetings
From the lorries battered all the breath out of me

But I do know, if I had, I'd have missed

A long quiet walk over the meseta;
Frost crisp underfoot; the sky an unbroken blue;
Larksong; watching my shadow slowly shorten
And edge towards the north; feeling my shoulders
Warm to the sun, and hearing that first cicada.

León

This, in my eyes, is the great cathedral.
Proof that actuality need not always
Be the impoverishment of what is possible.

In its Gothic fragility it holds back
From Baroque's magniloquent contempt for tact.

I sit and watch the shadows of the nesting storks.
Like holy ghosts, they rise and fall
Behind the stained-glass windows of the choir.

With three rose-windows, and over two
Hundred storied and decorated panes,
It sometimes seems that there's more glass than stone.

But late of an afternoon, when the sun
Rings in through these golds, these greens, these reds,
And through this lapis blue, it can feel

As though it is neither glass nor stone,
But the light itself that sustains it all.

Outside Villafranca del Bierzo

For a moment I felt like Robert Frost:
There being two roads to choose from,
But the one less-travelled-by
Looked private too.

              I stood there, uncertain
And conspicuous, and an old man in crumpled
Beret and carpet slippers came tottering
Towards me. 'Hola,' I said. 'Can I take
Either of these paths?'

             'How can I answer
Such a question,' he barked, 'when I don't know
Where you're going to, or why?'

             God damn it,
Another time warp: I'd gone and got myself
My own leech-gatherer now. Lost for words,
I took the Frost road in a rush and headed
For a fold in the hills.

             There was hibiscus
Growing there and I saw my first
Hoopoe, but could not shake
That old man from my mind. At every bend
In the turnings of my thought he came back at me,
Like some ancient Taoist, his beard
White now, his hands tucked inside his sleeves.
Sometimes he was positively Jungian.

One thing I could be sure of: he'd be waiting
To have another go at me on the way down.
But I'd get him this time. I'd be
On the other road for a start. And I was,
And so was he, jabbing the gravel with his stick.

It was a challenge, I knew that. 'Well?' he said.
'Absolutely marvellous,' I replied,
Trying to hint that he'd missed out on something,
Stuck down here beside his house all day.
Then, and this was my big ploy, adding
Enigmatically, 'And I have been
Where I have been.' I'd practised it. *He ido*
Adónde he ido. But he, with the gesture
Of one throwing a peseta to a beggar,
Said, 'Hombre, isn't that always the way?'

Dust

The rain has stopped now that I'm in Galicia,
And the mud-ruts in the lanes are baked and dried.
Even so, I keep on seeing that same
Bootprint. All the way from Pamplona
It's been with me; sometimes so fresh I've felt
Certain to meet up with whoever made it
Over the next hill, but never have.

What's one though, when this road is deep
With the footprints of the dead? Everywhere
You look, someone who went before has left
His mark: be it that little ivory crucifix
In León, whose Christ seemed quite contented
On his cross, smiling and wearing a skull-cap;
Or the great Gothic cathedrals themselves.

Each swirl of dust that clouds up round my feet
Assumes a separate and momentary shape.
Watching them, one might be led to think
That it was the spirit of the dust
That travelled, enhanced and quickened
Into something complex and more strange,
But falling, it settles and is dust again.

Exhausted or exultant, there is no avoiding
The ghosts of those who plodded along this road:
per lo cammino alto e silvestro.
Like them I cursed at the incessant rain
As I climbed up through the Pyrenees,
And knew the purgatory of seeming not to move
As I trekked across the high plains of Castille.

There are destinations which demand
That we ourselves have been the journey,
And it is some way yet to Santiago.
Maybe I've brought too much: guide books and maps
Can blur the edge of our uncertainties.
Travelling on with a trust in what was there,
They walked their faith. I walk their elegy.

At Samos: A Question

'And what wood are you made of, my son.'
It wasn't a question. I could tell that.
He was a Benedictine, and much taken
By my walking-stick: the slim, ebony

Look to it, and its sleek, swept-back
Dog's-head handle: sad-eyed and with a touch
Of the lugubrious about the jaw-line.
I had bought it in the Grand Bazaar

In Istanbul, and had myself been taken,
And taken in by it too. It wasn't
Until I got home I realised
That it was in fact just lacquered bamboo.

But I'd walked over three hundred miles with it
In three weeks, and the monk was impressed.
No, it wasn't a question. I knew that.
All the same, I wish he hadn't asked it.

A Dish of Scallops

Botticelli's Venus
comes surfboarding
coyly ashore on the most
famous scallop shell of all.
Scallops hood the porches of Queen
Anne doorways; form the backdrop to
Bernini's Triton Fountain; decorate
hemlines, necklines, and sarcophagi;
are the emblem of a chain of petrol
stations; and were they the only
sign out here on the Camino,
no one ever would their
true love know.

A young man's horse
bolted into the sea
and Saint James emerged
covered in shells, to rescue him
Pecten maximus, unlike other bivalves
is (fittingly) gregarious and mobile.
Threatened by starfish, 'the forcible
ejection of a jet of water throws the
animal in the other direction'. Oddly
an escalope is a slice of veal, but
coquille is wiselike (I'm sorry
I meant likewise) French
for a misprint.

At the Tomb of Saint James

Now whether his body is in the tomb or not
Is only a question of matter,
So scarcely matters, and it is hard to say

Whether the absence of his presence
Or the presence of his absence
Is now the more palpable;

Or whether it is the gathering
And gathered resonance of us all
That echoes and creates.

Endings

Now that I am here, I ask myself why.
        I had not expected
any kind of epiphany, knowing when I came
        to Mateo's
Portico de Gloria, that the smiles on the lips
        of the saints

would stay stony, the hurdy-gurdy dumb.
        I would, even so,
have welcomed a sign, if not of praise, at least
        of recognition
that something had happened. Was it different then
        for those who came

in their scallop hats and sandal shoon? Did they
        run all the way
from the top of Mount Joy, believing that below them
        lay the Heavenly City?
Was it for them not just a road but an allegory?
        It is tempting to think so.

In the hope that myth may sometimes define
        our intuitions
of reality, we are always happy to give house-room
        to any suggestion
that there is a point to what we are doing: a charm
        against the haphazard;

so the insinuations of travel become ever more Dantean:
        the cold and the wet
of the Pyrenees, that long trudge across the meseta,
        the deep green lanes of Galicia,
and finally a cathedral whose granite does seem
        to shimmer with gold-dust.

Still, this sense of let-down...Such reach of purpose
        hones awareness,
until you know that any final step would be
        a rehearsal
for death, but that is a step as resistant
        to metaphor as it is

to reason. We set out and we return. And we set out
        for something which never
has been reached, because to do so is to go beyond it,
        and we return
to something within us which has never come into being
        nor ever passed away.

All other offers of certainty are as evasive
        as those small
flurries and scatters of birds that keep drifting on
        just ahead of you
down the whole length of a hedgerow when you are
        out there walking.